Marsupials

Tasmanian Devils

by Natalie Deniston

Bullfrog Books

Ideas for Parents and Teachers

Bullfrog Books let children practice reading informational text at the earliest reading levels. Repetition, familiar words, and photo labels support early readers.

Before Reading
- Discuss the cover photo. What does it tell them?
- Look at the picture glossary together. Read and discuss the words.

Read the Book
- "Walk" through the book and look at the photos. Let the child ask questions. Point out the photo labels.
- Read the book to the child, or have them read independently.

After Reading
- Prompt the child to think more. Ask: Tasmanian devils are marsupials. Moms have pouches. Can you name any other marsupials?

Bullfrog Books are published by Jump!
5357 Penn Avenue South
Minneapolis, MN 55419
www.jumplibrary.com

Copyright © 2025 Jump! International copyright reserved in all countries. No part of this book may be reproduced in any form without written permission from the publisher.

Library of Congress Cataloging-in-Publication Data

Names: Deniston, Natalie, author.
Title: Tasmanian devils / by Natalie Deniston.
Description: Minneapolis, MN: Jump!, Inc., [2025]
Series: Marsupials | Includes index.
Audience: Ages 5–8
Identifiers: LCCN 2024020088 (print)
LCCN 2024020089 (ebook)
ISBN 9798892135283 (hardcover)
ISBN 9798892135290 (paperback)
ISBN 9798892135306 (ebook)
Subjects: LCSH: Tasmanian devil—Juvenile literature.
Classification: LCC QL737.M33 D46 2025 (print)
LCC QL737.M33 (ebook)
DDC 599.2/7—dc23/eng/20240506
LC record available at https://lccn.loc.gov/2024020088
LC ebook record available at https://lccn.loc.gov/2024020089

Editor: Katie Chanez
Designer: Emma Almgren-Bersie

Photo Credits: Gerry Pearce/Alamy, cover; ozflash/iStock, 1; Benny Marty/Shutterstock, 3; Dave Watts/Alamy, 4; PytyCzech/iStock, 5; Dave Watts/Nature Picture Library, 6–7, 23br; Auscape International Pty Ltd/Alamy, 8–9, 23bl; imageBROKER.com GmbH & Co. KG/Alamy, 10, 22; Photoshot - NHPA/SuperStock, 11, 23tl; slowmotiongli/iStock, 12–13; CraigRJD/iStock, 14; Benny Marty/Alamy, 15; TonyFeder/iStock, 16–17, 23tr; Susan Flashman/Shutterstock, 18–19; keiichihiki/iStock, 20–21; Frank Martins/Shutterstock, 24.

Printed in the United States of America at Corporate Graphics in North Mankato, Minnesota.

Table of Contents

In the Pouch	4
Parts of a Tasmanian Devil	22
Picture Glossary	23
Index	24
To Learn More	24

In the Pouch

Look! Tasmanian devils!

Mom has a pouch.

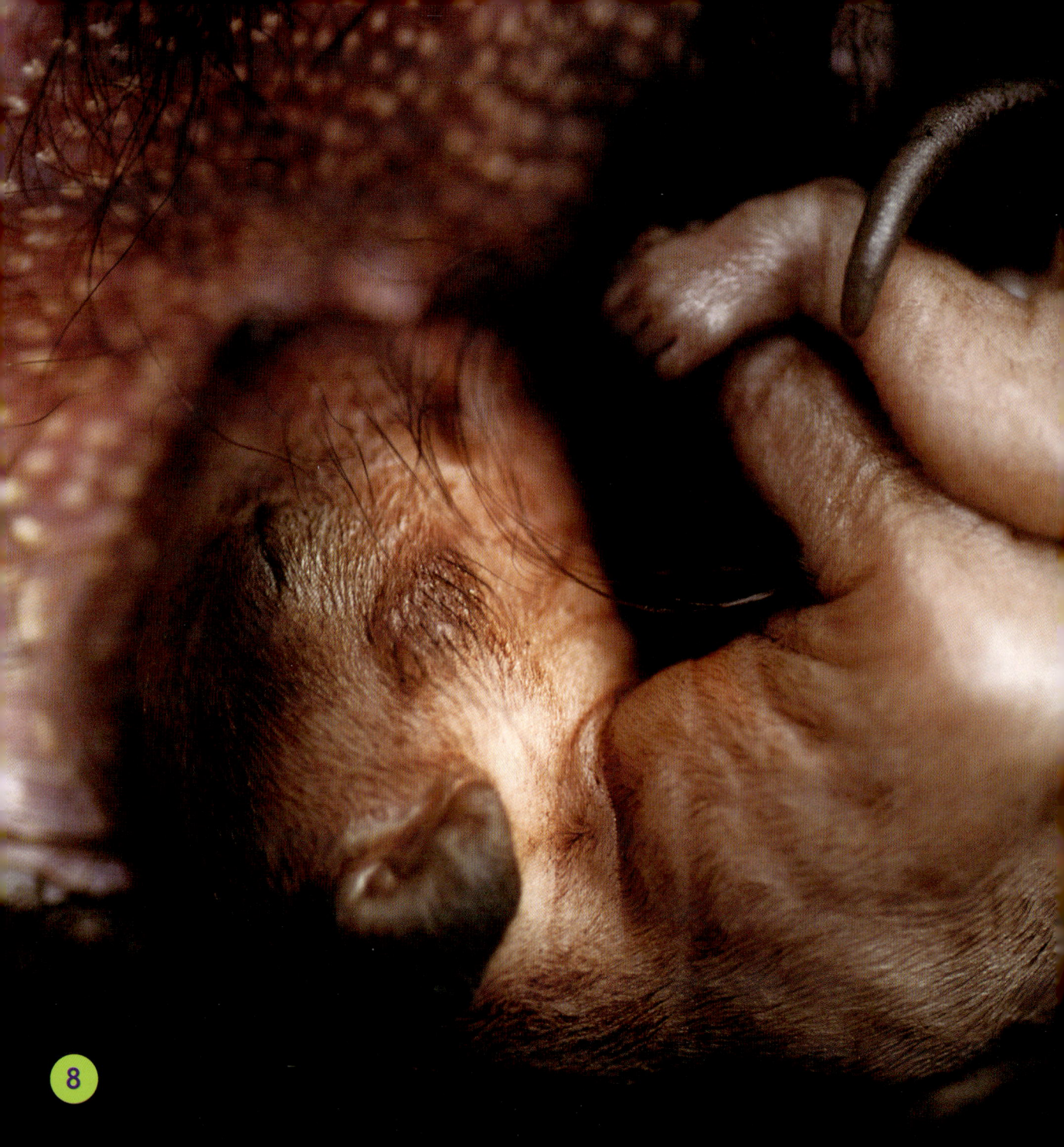

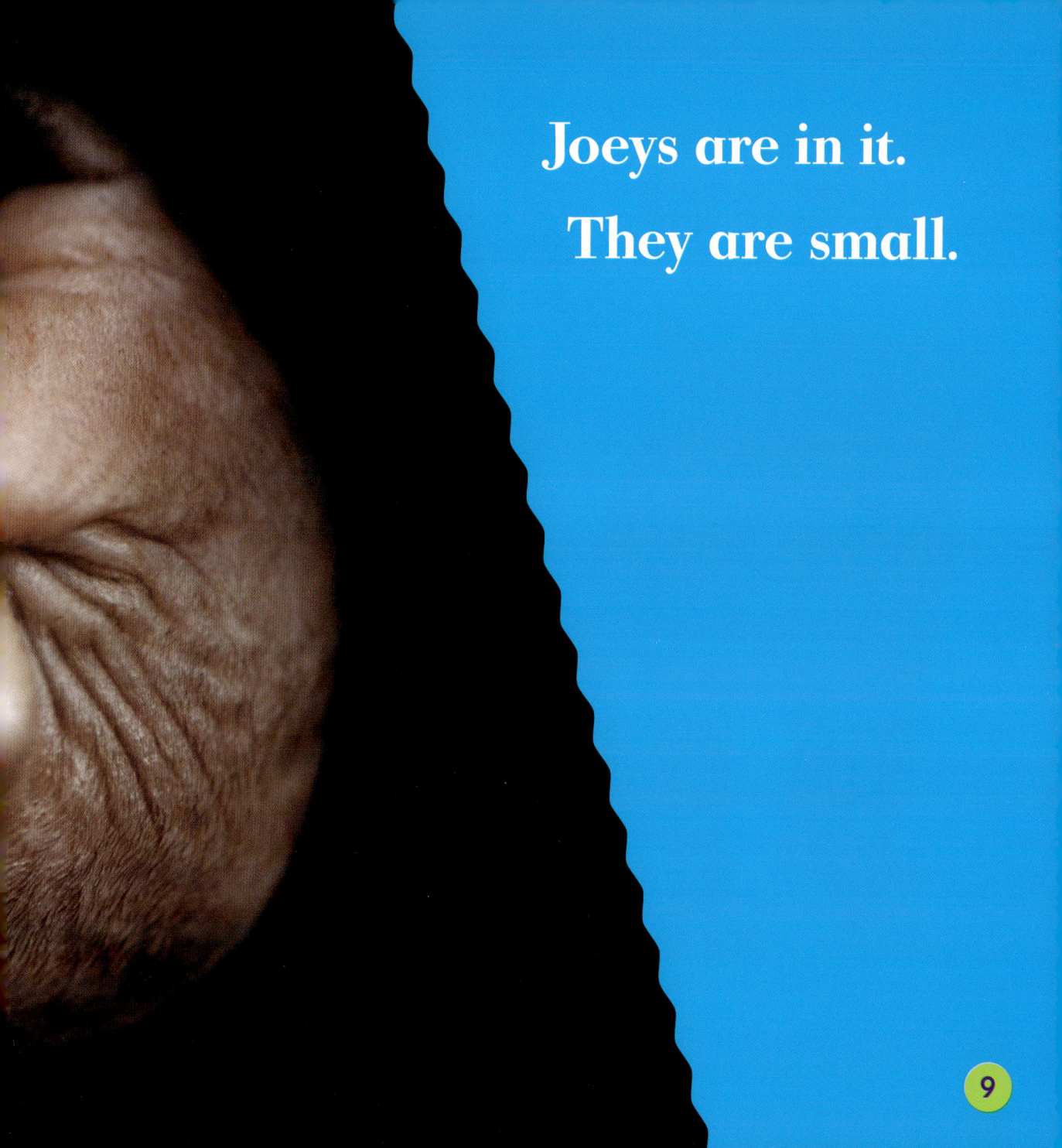

Joeys are in it.

They are small.

They grow.

They live in a den.

They grow up!
They come out at night.
Why?
They look for food.

Like what?
Dead animals.
Ew!

They all want to eat.

He will not share.

He howls.

He shows his teeth.

They fight!

No one is hurt.
It is morning.
They sleep.

Parts of a Tasmanian Devil

What are the parts of a Tasmanian devil? Take a look!

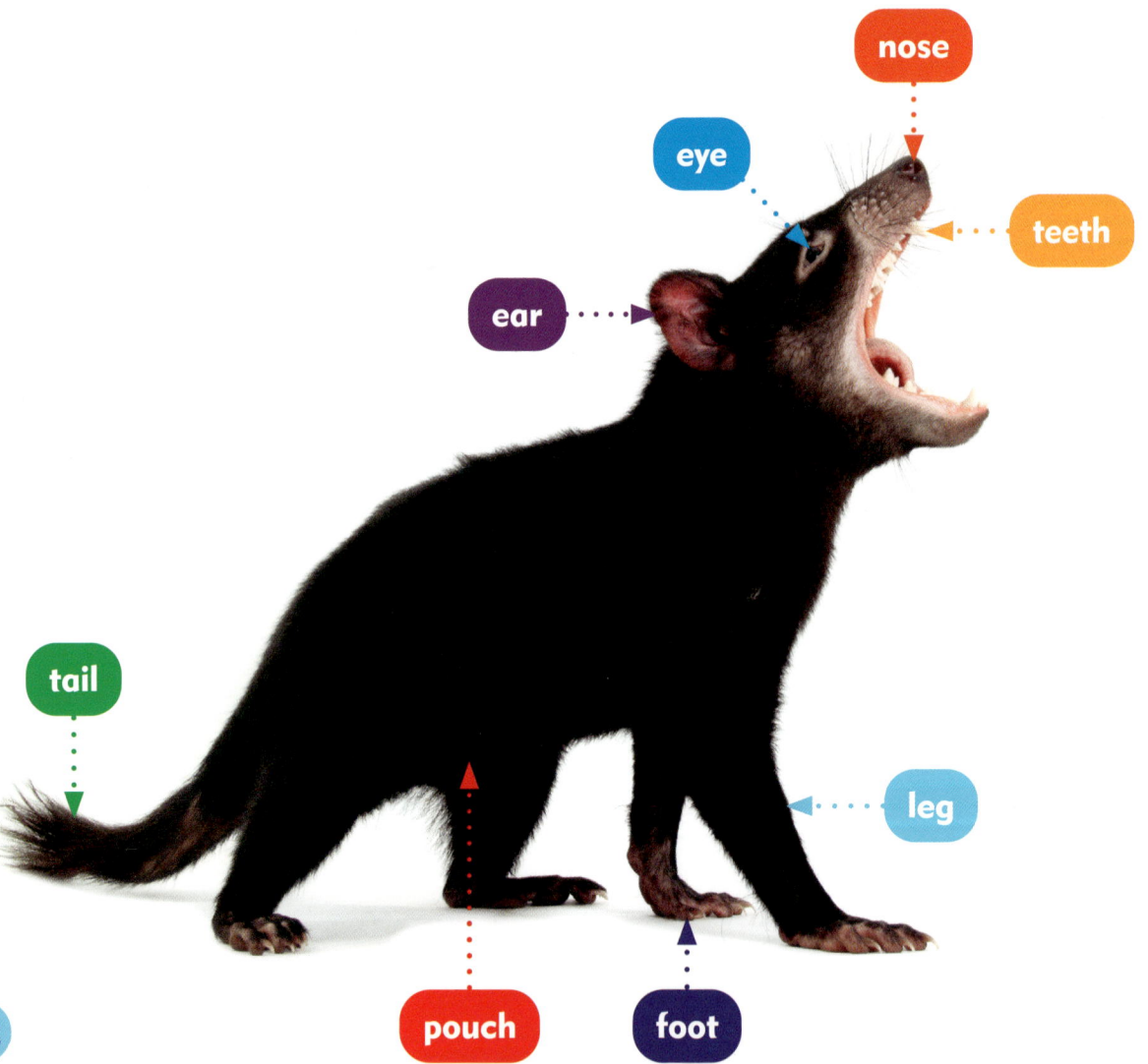

Picture Glossary

den
The home of a wild animal.

howls
Makes a long, loud cry.

joeys
Baby Tasmanian devils.

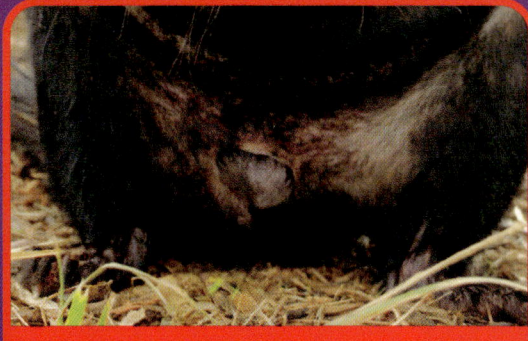

pouch
A pocket in a marsupial mother's body in which it carries its young.

Index

dead animals 14
den 11
eat 15
fight 19
food 13
grow 10, 13
howls 16
joeys 9
night 13
pouch 6
sleep 20
teeth 16

To Learn More

Finding more information is as easy as 1, 2, 3.
❶ Go to www.factsurfer.com
❷ Enter "Tasmaniandevils" into the search box.
❸ Choose your book to see a list of websites.